THE COMMON PARTY

CONTENTS

PREAMBLE

At the founding of the United States, our first President George Washington bode farewell to this nation, warning us of the dangers of parties, where it begins to limit the nature of free thought itself.

With the modern political system, the common man is forced to decide between extremes and must go with the party that they dislike the least. There is only a duality within the modern voting system, which can hardly be called modern with its ever increasing age. The modern politician, who claims to be a common man himself, becomes merely a symbol of the dangers of party alignment, having to extremize more and more to appeal to the most zealous voters.

This zealousness within our political system has turned into a toxic mess, where both sides blame the other of the same offenses, though it is only them who vote.

We believe in giving the common man a proper say, one to give reason and benefit the middle of society. So often is the middle just ignored even though most of the populace falls under there.

We do not believe in extremes and believe that instead of the government squabbling over what should be non-issues such as the freedom of the modern internet from corporate control, the government should think of the future before it rests upon us, with its countless issues such as artificial intelligence, automation of the workforce, and the future of this great nation.

But the issue of the polarization of party grows, especially since the beginning of the 21st century. We have seen parties grow more extreme, with a larger proportion of the base becoming unrepresented unless they change their viewpoints to match the party as well. This control undermines the point of party: the people of the party must control the party, not vice versa. Multipartisanship must take place for the government to be properly be ruled by the people.

As the political spectrum more approaches a horseshoe instead of a straight line, with both far left and far right posing one extreme, the other end, with proper common sense, must be represented properly in the evolving democracy in the United States of America, and by forming this Common Party, we, as Americans, can make extinguish the every growing polarization in this great nation.

BUDGET

The United States has gained the majority of its grounds as the world's leading superpower through programs such as NASA, EPA, CIA and others dedicated to making the world a better place. The Common Party believes that the national budget has become skewed with unnecessarily large amounts of money and resources being misspent in various areas. The Party believes that the national budget should be funneled towards programs that meet the following criteria: 1) Benefit the nation and the world 2) Benefit other national programs and/or 3) Public need at the time.

MILITARY AND SCIENCE BUDGET

As the years roll by, the budget of the military of the United States has gradually increased to a staggering amount with no indications of going back down but rather continuing to go up. The extra investments into the military are going into research and development of new technologies that are being designed to destroy our enemies. However, as the budget for the military increases, the budget for science is decreasing. Across the board, scientific agencies such as the NASA and CDC are losing the financial means to sustain what they are accomplishing. In combination, these two sectors, the military and science, are indeed creating a negative effect on one another. Scientific institutions generate new technologies in the wake of their exploration for the truth and these developments are able to be used for military purposes. However, when the military develops a new technology, that technology is kept secret from the rest of the world and this has the potential to harm the United States when it come to science when compared with the rest of the world. The Common Party believes that more money should be taken away from the military and given to scientific agencies in order to create a more sustainable and mutual bond between the institutions.

AUTOMATION AND THE FUTURE OF THE WORKPLACE

Modern technology and its eventual outcomes pose an apparent "threat" to many jobs in the workplace in the form of automation but the Common Party embraces this future. It is not a matter of if corporations will automate but simply a matter of when. The Automation of Corporate America Agency will usher in a new era of automation in the workplace and mediate the transition for both the business and the workers. A department will be organized to investigate and assist businesses in replacing workers with automated machines wherever possible. The automation of the workplace will be a government mandate and any entity that does not comply will be heavily fined, which will be equal to the amount they pay their employees in total.

The Automation of Corporate America Agency will then evaluate every three years how much each entity is saving through automation and then create a filing that will tax the entity only 30% of the savings, which excludes the running cost of the automation, every year until the next evaluation. This money will go directly into the Universal Basic Income Program to help compensate workers who have been replaced and allow them to eventually return to the workforce.

UNIVERSAL BASIC INCOME

In regards to the opinion of the Common Party, the welfare system should be replaced by the Universal Basic Income Program. This program will provide those who make a salary that amounts less than $100,000 (adjusted for inflation from the year 2020), with that of the poverty level income over a twelve month period through equal monthly payments for those who are at voting age. The use of this money will be left up to the individual.

A Universal Basic Income Program allows for an individual to leave their current place of employment which they may detest and go back to a place of higher learning so that once they return to the workforce they can work higher level or more self satisfying jobs.

Without the fear of living with no income, workers are able to stand up for their rights and not have the fear of being fired and left without a lifeline, a fate that many face during times of economic turmoil and possibly during unregulated automation.

This accomplishes a freedom of choice that all Americans should have.

UNEMPLOYMENT ELIMINATION PROGRAM

The Unemployment Elimination Program will assist the unemployed in gaining jobs or going back to school to gain new skills to benefit both themselves and society. The program will also create outlines for how people spend their money until they get back on their feet.

The program will help unemployed citizens dress professionally and will provide basic necessities until the unemployed are back on their feet. To be a part of the program, people must prove that they are continuously looking for new jobs as well as applying.

BUSINESS FOUNDING CENTERS

Centers will be erected in each state's capital with satellite buildings being set up around other population centers of states with the main center near Washington D.C.. These centers will be directed to help people through the process of creating and maintaining a business and obtaining permits and licenses needed on both federal and state levels.

This will be greatly beneficial to those who wish to create a new business but find the process and the mounds of paperwork daunting. To the individual creating the business, the process will appear more streamlined.

INNOVATION

The Common Party believes that innovation is the key to the future and how this great nation will remain an economic and scientific powerhouse, a facet that spawned America's greatest inventions such as the electric light bulb and the modern automobile. The Common Party advocates for the creation of the Innovation Task Force that will monitor corporations and patents and search for innovations being made, including, but not limited, to processes, products, and genetic modifications.

This task force will then recommend legislation that should greatly be considered as to how this innovation should become the new legal standard.

This task force will be most important when it comes to both human and environmental safety innovations. When the task force reveals an innovation in anything that pertains to these concerns, it will recommend legislation that makes anything less safe (to a significant degree) than the innovation illegal.

The recommendations on legislation will be brought to both houses of Congress allowing it to become full legislation as well as to the President who could act on the recommendation and create an Executive Order enforcing it.

AMERICAN ENERGY

The Common Party is a strong proponent of bringing back American energy. The Party believes that America should work towards being energy independent of other countries with the long term goal being to provide energy to other countries.

The Party also believes that more steps should be taken towards renewable energy in the forms of wind, hydroelectric, solar, and geothermal, where work to develop new technologies to harness these renewable resources will be heavily funded by the government, which will create a large amount of employment opportunities. The world as a whole must wean itself off of nonrenewable energy, and the United States must take its fair step in accomplishing that goal.

TAXES

The taxation system must be reworked in a rapidly changing economy especially with the ever-encroaching issues of the future. In an America with the Universal Basic Income Program, the income itself would not be taxed.

The Common Party supports a graduated income tax that is fair to all income levels and not excessive. However, the income tax should be more strongly enforced particularly on higher income brackets where money earned from America is not siphoned out to other nations be unused by those who would particularly require it due to governmental programs here in the United States.

The Party is also a proponent for allowing certain deductions on a citizens taxes but not having a large amount of deduction possibilities in place as to not allow an individual to circumvent the system and pay no taxes. The deductions that The Common Party support are those on work-related expenses, charitable donations, or the cost of dependent entities for a taxpayer.

WEALTH TAX

As The Common Party supports a fair and balanced taxation system in the United States, The Party supports the idea of a non-radical wealth tax. The Party believes that a wealth tax should be put in place on those who make $10,000,000 or more per year. This wealth tax, The Party believes, should be a 35% tax on the income plus a 10% optional tax. The optional tax is a tax in which the taxpayer gets to decide where the money goes. The ways that the taxpayer may fulfill the requirements of the optional tax are by donating to a charity, investing into infrastructure, investing into a company whether it be their own or someone else's, or by paying the government as they would with their other tax dollars. Any combination of expenditures that follow these requirements that adds up to 10% of the individual's income will satisfy the optional tax.

The Party also believes that the government should also consider an optional tax for other income brackets.

INTERNATIONAL TRADE

The Common Party is a strong proponent for an fairly open trade system with an emphasis on fair deals alongside the freedom to make such transactions. It is our belief that America should not begin a trade war with foreign entities due to the ever-increasing interconnected nature of a global economy and should attempt to maintain both simplicity and equality within the international marketplace.

It is the party's belief that tariffs on imports should be minimized enough so that ports can operate with a reasonable amount of profit while also maintaining a high amount of international trade.

These ideals embody the exchange of ideas which the Common Party believes should be open, allowing people from all walks of life, from economic to social to national backgrounds, to freely discuss ideas and ideals to improve our democracy in the marketplace of ideas.

SENSELESS WARS

The United States of America shall not involve itself in wars over oil or continue on campaigns that are not going to work due to outdated tactics.

To the first point, as the United States should focus on remaining renewably energy independent, The Party believes that the United States should no longer fight wars over natural resources.

To the second point, the United States has waged many wars and has used the same fighting tactics with no avail. This has led to the wars lasting forever and it is the belief of The Party that if there is no substantial reason for the country to be risking the lives of its citizens then the United States should pull out.

EQUALITY

The United States of America did not start as an equal environment for the people who live in it, and it still does not uphold the self-evident truth of equality for all. Ever since the end of slavery, it still took 100 years to try and level the field between races, which has been incredibly detrimental to the ideals of democracy.

These attempts, however, have failed to succeed with race disparities leading to many outrageous disparities in wealth and education.

The Common Party is focused on ending this lasting inequality, which does not simply exist with race; it includes gender, religion, and sexuality as well. It unfairly divides many people who would otherwise agree on beliefs that may be more important than small qualifiers which separate them. Equality between groups must be not just promoted, it must be realized as no person can be superior to any other, for we are all just people.

SECURITY OF THE NATION AND THE INDIVIDUAL

The nature of globalism is a double-edged sword; it exposes this nation to many new ideas and products with the benefit of free trade, but some ideas may be incredibly harmful to political discourse especially with those focused on bringing terror to further their cause.

Of course, government agencies are in place to help prevent instances of terrorism, but a fragile balance must be forged and maintained between privacy and protection, especially in a world where the privacies of the individual can be exposed with much more ease.

Cyberterrorism is more prominent of a threat in the modern day and age where so much incredibly sensitive information is stored in the internet where breaches of privacy and infrastructure can be so much easier with far larger consequences. The government must put graver consequences on these large data breaches on both the group who breaches and the group that is breached in order to ensure other similar events cannot happen.

The government should also spend more time to educate the older members of government on how exactly technology and technological companies function so that they can better govern and oversee them. The government should not be working against these companies but rather with them.

The Common Party believes that government agencies must be partially repurposed and expanded to protect the individual as well from external threats, both domestic and international, and ensure the welfare of the people in this age where technology is gaining an ever-important role in modern society.

PRESERVATION OF THE ENVIRONMENT

The National Parks System has an incredibly important role in preserving the natural beauties of America, from Yosemite to Acadia. Not only should their role in preservation be maintained, their role in educating the populace about should still be present and reinforced. These beauties of the United States of America must be preserved at all cost and will not be reduced in size at any point in time.

Regarding a general view on environmental preservation, corporations should refocus from a utilization of nonrenewable resources and thus unsustainable practices to that of a maintainable nature. The Common Party will support the research and development departments of companies that focus on resources of nonrenewable nature through grants with the sole goal of either maximum reduction of waste or total shift from nonrenewable practices to renewable, i.e. shifting the plastics industry from its crude oil dependency to bioplastics.

Climate change is very much a real issue, with overwhelming amounts of evidence suggesting so. The Common Party is in full support of reducing carbon emissions, which have proven to be a major culprit in climate change. Regarding mass extinctions, it has never been about the mere amount of carbon in the atmosphere; rather, mass extinctions have occurred due to a large shift of rate of carbon emission into the environment, which is a trend apparent in geological data.

The Party believes that the United States should not be pressured to follow other countries in their efforts to combat climate change but should rather be the ones pressuring other countries to follow in its footsteps.

EDUCATION OF THE NEXT GENERATION

The Common Party believes that the current education system should be reformed to incorporate a more personalized experience for each student. Students will be able to begin to choose between STEM and Humanities fields as early as ninth grade, allowing them to begin to achieve a more specialized skill set from an earlier age. This will reduce the number of general course requirements for students, allowing them to focus their efforts on what truly interests them, hopefully encouraging learning, rather than diminishing children's love of learning. However this will not limit their ability to change their major in the future.

The education system should also be reformed to not just teach students information so that they may regurgitate it but rather teach students the methods of free and critical thinking.

Regarding higher education, the government must ensure some lowered tuition to prevent those seeking to better themselves from entrapping themselves in large amounts of debt.

TEACHER SALARIES

The Common Party believes that it is in the best interest of society that teacher salary shall be based upon the teacher's performance especially with the resources that they are granted instead of solely tenure. The methods by which how the teacher's performance shall be judged, how cheating shall be counteracted, and how the teacher's performance equates to pay shall be left up to the individual states.

This method of determining salary serves as encouragement for teachers to maximize productivity the classroom environment.

DRIVER'S LICENSES

It is the belief of the party that drivers shall be required by national law to retake a driving test every 12 years after gaining their first full drivers license. There will be no exceptions to anyone which means that everyone, no matter what age, will be taking the same test with the same requirements.

This will prevent drivers who have become dangerous on the road from being on the road thus increasing public safety.

THE MODIFICATION OF THE HEALTHCARE SYSTEM

Healthcare has been dramatically changing over the past years and the common person is becoming more vulnerable to predatory practices by corporations to save their own health. The Common

Party believes in the creation of a new governmental agency to monitor the actions of both health insurance companies and hospitals to ensure that healthcare is affordable and especially that medical costs are not excessive, which is particularly important to an uninsured person to not place them in extreme amounts of debt.

This agency would primarily monitor hospitals and costs of various items to an uninsured patient. If the individual costs of said items appear extremely unreasonable to the common person, the description of the unreasonably priced object will be closely scrutinized in order to check if there is a valid reason for said pricing. If there is no valid reason, the hospital must reduce its cost to a reasonable amount.

The Party also believes that coverage for pre-existing conditions shall be protected.

Regarding private health insurance agencies, the agency must simply check whether they are price gouging after the reduced raw medical cost.

MARIJUANA

Marijuana was first made illegal as a need for a man to keep a job. When prohibition was ended, the man in charge of enforcing it was faced with the loss of a job and decided that his best course of action was to find another substance to ban. He turned to racism and said that marijuana was making Mexicans lazy and that was destroying the United States. This stuck and, ever since, the United States has increased its criminalization of the substance on the federal level.

The Common Party wishes to completely decriminalize marijuana is all of its forms and allow the substance back into the marketplace. The Party also holds firm that this action will greatly strengthen the economy and provide more tax revenue.

IMMIGRATION

Immigration has been a contentious issue especially since the post-war era. The Common Party's stance on immigration is simple: preserve the current system as it is already very strict regarding visas and all those who have visas for over 6 months must take a 3-week crash course in American culture and laws within their first sixth months.

Families of immigrants shall not be ripped apart and thrown into an unforgiving environment only because they wanted to make their lives better or merely safe. Indeed, The Party holds true the belief that more areas of entry should be established as to allow for immigrants to cross into the country safely and responsibly. The Common Party does not believe that potential immigrants should have to run miles beside a wall or avoid airport security while running from murderers, rapists, or extortionist OR live in the United States with the fear that if they try to gain citizenship that they will be sent back to these people.

The United States was built on the principles of being a safe haven for the world so the idea that the United States would turn away people in need is outrageous. The Common Party is also entirely supportive of accepting asylum-seekers or those seeking refuge from their country of origin (with thorough checking of validity of claims).

REFORMATION OF THE CRIMINAL JUSTICE SYSTEM

The Common Party is an advocate for a large reform of the current criminal processing system, where all jails and prisons should not be privately held enterprises but instead be run by the appropriate government. The system should also focus on a rehabilitation of criminals to ensure they become a working member of society once more after release, where they will be assisted in gaining employment through systems detailed previously.

Ex-felons, however, must prove to be functional members of society as well as showing absolutely no tendency to revert back to felonious ways alongside approval by a local mental health institution to be eligible for benefits.

Ex-convicts, The Party believes, should also be given back their rights such as the right to vote.

PRESIDENTIAL POWER

The Common Party holds the belief that, while the president does hold many powers, the president is not able to self pardon or obstruct justice in any means including firing the lead investigator into an investigation on him or herself. They do not have to power to pardon themselves or given security clearance against the wishes of top officials. The president has the power to direct certain agencies and write executive orders to dictate their responsibilities but does not have the right to override the an agency when the override may destroy the agency. Only by a vote of congress can an agency be shut down.

MONEY IN POLITICS

The Common Party holds firmly to the belief that money does not belong in politics. The Party believes that special interest should not be allowed to persuade individuals to a certain candidate and should not be permitted to influence a politicians vote through what is essentially bribery. These actions shall be barred and met with severe consequences. Private citizens should be the only ones allowed to contribute, not groups with special connections.

FREEDOM OF SPEECH, RELIGION, AND THE PRESS

The Common Party is a full supporter of the constitutional right to freedom of speech, religion, and the press, especially on the internet, which is proving to be an influential forum for people to discuss. The party also believes in a complete separation of religion and the government, where they really should not be affecting each other at all, and the government should not be under the influence of any religion.

WOMANS' REPRODUCTIVE RIGHTS

The Common Party holds the ideal that the right to abortion must remain protected. The chose of whether to have an abortion is up to the woman who is carrying the fetus; with the exception of the doctor performing an abortion when the life of the woman is at risk. As a fetus does not begin to establish a sense of pain until the third trimester, the mother may have an abortion with no questions asked in the first two trimesters and may only have an abortion in the last trimester if her health is compromised.

THE RIGHT TO BEAR ARMS

The Common Party believes that no firearm, whether single-shot or fully automatic, or firearm accessory shall ever be restricted or banned from the marketplace as a protection of the Second Amendment of the Constitution of the United States. Firearms shall not be restricted in any public or private space with the only place where possession can be limited being government facilities. While firearms possession cannot be restricted in public spaces, they must be concealed as to not instill fear in others, and the choice of concealment will be up to the discretion of the owner of a private space. This means that all non concealable firearms must be kept within cars or homes and may only be transported in a way that is not obvious.

To be eligible for firearm ownership, the Party believes, one must possess a high-school diploma or GED. One will also have to pass a gun safety and responsibility course that will last 90 days that can either be taken in high-school (which will be required for every school to offer) or later in life. An abbreviated seminar will need to be taken and passed again after 7 years of originally passing the course. Then, when purchasing a firearm, one will have to pass a comprehensive background check.

However, the Party does believe one's eligibility for firearm ownership should be lost if they are involved in any criminal activity. They can obtain their eligibility back by 1) retaking and getting a 90% or more on a gun safety and responsibility course that last 90 days (consecutive or non-consecutive) and 2) proving themselves to and performing any additional punishment assigned by the judge who originally oversaw the case in which they were prosecuted.

However, the Party does not advocate for the right for ex-felons to regain the right to bear arms.

The Firearm Ownership Agency should be created to maintain databases of individuals who have taken and passed the gun safety and responsibility course, when the individuals need to take the abbreviated seminar, who has had their rights stripped, and run background checks. The agency will also regulate these processes and create the outline for the gun safety and responsibility course and the abbreviated seminar. The agency will do all of this within the limits outlined in the above paragraphs.

VOTING RIGHT

The Common Party advocates for an alternative voting system which would allow for people to not solely have to vote for someone they like the least but instead for people who they more agree with. It is also the Party's belief that a candidate should have to receive a large majority of votes to win so that the least amount of people are unhappy.

The Party also believes in the complete abolishment of the Electoral College.

VACCINATIONS

The Common Party supports science and innovation in all of its endeavors and believes that vaccinations are one of the greatest inventions of all of history. Vaccinations have increased the life span and have allowed people to save large sums of money on hospital bills. However, there is a growing threat called the anti-vaxxer movement. This movement is seeking to undermine science and the safety of children. Through not vaccinating one's child, the parents are not only putting their child in harms way but they are putting every person that their child comes in contact with in danger.

The Party believes that swift action needs to be taken against this dangerous movement. To do this, The Party supports an action that would declare the act of not vaccinating one's child as child endangerment. The Party also supports private institutions from barring individuals who do not have vaccinations from stepping on their grounds.

After these actions take affect, The Party understands that some doctors will falsify records for certain unvaccinated individuals and because of this the punishment for falsifying records should be severe.

HATE GROUPS

Hate groups are defined as groups of people that believe in certain principles that separate themselves from other individuals on the basis of religion, race, gender, etc. These groups have strong influence and can lead to great acts of violence taking place. These acts can range from a murder to a genocide.

The Common Party believes that a sitting president, justice, or congressman/congresswoman should be required to denounce these groups during inauguration and that no bills that support these groups should be allowed to be written in law.

The Party does acknowledge that these groups can not be silenced as that is a violation of their constitutional rights but does believe that private companies such as Facebook and Google should take action to cut of the groups' connections to impressionable individuals who may take up violent action.

INTERNET ACCESS

The internet has become a vital part of life and if one is left without it for even a week they miss so much. Without the internet, some individuals may not be able to work or to research each political candidate before voting. The Common Party believes that action needs to be taken to give access to the internet to low income individuals as well as those who live in remote communities. These actions will serve to unite the United States even more as well as allow for even more intellectual and physical trade.

The Party also holds true the ideals of a free and open internet and that internet providers do not have the right to throttle certain webpages based off of how much the webpage owner pays the provider or how much the provider agrees with the content. The Party believes that providers only have the right to block certain webpages that contain dangerous material such as webpages belonging to the KKK.

The Party also supports an individuals right to research information on many political ideals whether they be for a specific party or even a different form of government such as communism. It is through this research that an individual form an opinion and allows for open dialogue and a better search for the right way to govern.